Rare Bird

TREVI BENNETT

Inquiries for reprint permission to: PO Box 1335 Aspen CO 81612 or kayarebel@me.com

Summary: Poetry is an expression of the moment and a glimpse into the emotion of the author. The reader is invited to dive into the juxtaposition and play on words.

Rare Bird by Trevi Bennett – Volume 2

ISBN-13: 978-0615580777 (Trevi Bennett)

First printing 2012
The text for this book is set in Verdana

[Body, Mind & Spirit / Inspiration & Personal Growth]

LOVINGLY DEDICATED TO

Leona and Robert Moore

ACKNOWLEDGMENTS

Endless thanks to my friend Shannon Clare who assisted in editing my first million rounds of my book. Shannon, you successfully inspired me to express my creativity. Finally, letting it all flow, I thank you tons.

I wish to empower healing in each individual. This is possible for everyone by simply starting now and expressing yourself by any means. Everything qualifies as art, so make your daily rituals an art form.

I am also thankful for the tireless work and witty jaunts of Christina Oxenberg who is blazing the trail for young authors everywhere. Christina, you weave magic one word at a time.

Giving is the simplest form of receiving and sharing is the simplest form of giving. Think about what you want and vibrate on that level.

SICKLY SWEET SMELL DELUSION

Unwary unwilling unable

Extricate illusion unstable

Remembering redundancies

Recalling favors

Hoping hypocrisy hollow

Fear fading

Frantically follow

Hard hurting self hindrances

APPLY VANITIES

Expert hands

Versed regime

Ulterior plan

Ideas acceptance

Limit perception

Perpetuate rejection

Apply insanities

Symptoms cause

Battling demon

We never saw

Too much free time

Sit with yourself

Look to someone else

Waiting for you to be you

And me to be me

RUNNING TIME

Before lost

Without afraid

Strange scarcity

Truth reverse

Love known

Flowers flee

To flight

Undiscovered reaction

Memory muscle

Defy odds

Recall strength

Discipline knot

Worry be

Your guide

ALIEN TOUCH

Vanquish every

Stall jabber

Filled empty

Sense fleeing

Means condensation

Freeing falling

Cerebral instinct

Intent feeling

Incomplete Alpha

Sprout manna

Serve master

Killer hasty

Alert content

OPEN EYES BEAMING

All knowing nose hearing

Ears feeling senses reeling

Fine kisses wind

Divine rays life

Growing soul stop go

Humming wheels float by

Propel I

Ever strong fight

Good versus right

Winged birds weather

Should live together

Sensi-bly high

Plant seeds change

Allow rearrange

Recognize self

Tap into wealth

WHICH PATH WILL YOU FOLLOW

That won't leave you hollow

No concept gain

No feeling pain

Awaiting fate

Running late

Hide run away

Or can I make you stay

Product life

Cut knife

Four directions mind

Labels discouragement

Apathy encouragement

Accept conquer

Seek find

Clear see fool

False things do

Free up let go

Fly high swing low

Wake up sweat

Found me yet

Didn't groove

Couldn't move

Fear unknown

Being alone

No concept time

No feeling rhyme

SIDE FLIP OPPOSITE

Backward upside down

Poise picture display

True actuality dismay

Limited quality last deal

Make life real

Encourage excel

Trail smell

Four ways follow

Lead to an end

Held close bay

Sculpture no clay

Swallow thrive

Choke on day

LOYAL FAITH BLESSED

Struggle might suffer fight

Free strife moving light

Soul spirit sprite

Open truth dignity

Seek peace teach life

Honor calm conscious

Rhyme change season

Reason wait time might

Bend brake bright

DOWN AWAY

Lack dismay

Time blind

Pain traps mind

Behind doors

Ungrateful scores

Seemingly kind

Wait rewind

Unfold defeat mass

Sweet mental cast

Loops bound ahead

Torment fled

Skip back feet

Whip crack fleet

TWO SAVANT

Conditioned constraints

Creative judgment

Limiting space

Mission Earth

Encourage self worth

Theory race

Excuse erase

There is fruit

Harvest truth

Desire wants get paid

Distractions fade

Potential grows

Effortlessly probability slows

HEAR BODY CRACK

Tears held back

Hold tight

Lurking past

Uncover soul

Breathe life whole

Wandering mind

Creative inspiration

Ego wastes time

Potential livication

Feel dark heart

Accept must part

Release deal

FORWARD RHYME

Puppet strings

Unleash wings

Loving life

Loose slack

Journeys seen

Bags pack

Young fact

Believe dreams

Impulsive rash

WAITING FLIRTING FINISH

Eyes halt hands

Wish I weren't wish I were

Once love close at hand

Call his lips mine own salvage

Love wrench logic

Ball of knowledge

Ever expanding strand

Previous eyes oblivion

Depth chocolate binge

Dose love day

Self hate kills all

Ended times can count

It's over echoing empty heart

Hollow never more fulfilling

Utter annoyance control

CRACKED TORN TIMES

Choosing one over another

Ignoring sister and brother

Keep it to yourself

Excuse to race

Water finds pace

Stretch forget

Start again

Sounds describe

Hoping lends

Trees can bend

Try not to try

Be here when you die

Second guess

Play pawn

Dodging fear

Telling lies

KICKING REALITY

Impermanent space

Spinning illusions

I-tinual place

Removing obstacles

Corners mind

Shoulds of a life

Reflecting I find

Beauty out tonight

Clear cut in

Paralyzed fear

Mesmerized hear

Confusing mine

Get in line

FALL OUT DROP IN

Ground or float

Stream flowing uncontrolled

River feels no pain

Drops trillions of rain

Hitting currents

Stuck between trapped

Moments burn

Eyes sensation

Holding back

Encourage delusion

Sew love

Fall the drop

Rock under water

TEARING STRANDS

Life bent fear

Fated exempt

Loud kittens

Warm hands healing

Tempted unearthed

Rearranged sunshine

Better than not well

Tomorrow undiluted

Wise poly-makers

Molded truth

Ice burning eyes

Not withholding

Given three no more

Less of tests to score

WHOLE PEOPLE WAITING

Half a life to live

Ole people waiting

Have a life to live

Why people waiting

All their lives to give

TOUCHING LIFE

Accepting high

Back on search

Almost slight

Forget strife

Lift burden light

More rough than right

FREE THOUGHTS

Changing Flow

Flying emotions

Static feelings

Fearful conditions

Soften forgiven

Wicking words

Picking birds

Licking wounds

Impermeable permanence

Inexplicable unavoidable

Inexhaustible

NOT GOING TO WAIT

Anymore you said

Need someone too

Alleviate fear

Party fine

Mess unwind

What's your plan you said

Heart made of lead

Unable to think

Heat escapes lips

Love is thick

Makes me sick

Same with lame hits

Held far from soul

Your mirror mine

Are we not the same

Escape again mind

Evaporating time

Where to look

How to feel

I don't understand you said

Eyes fixed

Feeling dead

Not realizing

Sensation life

Pull twist careless strife

One more moment can't stand

Up straight down demand

Memories endless time

Sore eyes sight

Leaving more light

Demands gone

Recall times we played

Together again

Not the same as before

STRONG SIMPLICITY CRACK TEAR

Delicate petals shake smear

Flapping silence move wind

Elevate shadows of wings

Elaborate selves absorb flock

Steamy mist circles lock

Yellow turn blue pixels day

Rest then rise then rest

Extended impatience my way

HALF BACK WHOLE HEART

Touch heal much

Kiss cheek weak

Long time gone

Now I know

Dunked strife

Punked life

Grind time wind line

Control pain release gain

Tension joy emotion coy

Inability flies fear dies

Sink self discover wealth

Soul light shine

Abundantly inextricably fine

TURN BACK

Babylon mainstream

Revisit dream

Rainbow Zion

Deny hypocrite

Intrinsically linked

Ideal benefit sees

Colors some lack

Voice opinion

Phoenix rising

Spectral light

MIND IS MEANS TOO

Draw upon lean on you

Ever forward fights

Stand firm rights

One people split

Two parties fit

Giving power to it

Lifting heads high

Focus ask why

Open eyes

Shift concepts change

Mind's emptiness

Increases range

EVOLVE OR DIE

The world is one tribe with a single consciousness. Realize that benefitting oneself is the quickest means to benefitting others. By strengthening your own vibration it is easy to then share that energy with those around you. The population of the world in 2012 is now over 7 billion people, effortlessly evolving with the rest of the planet.

ABOUT THE AUTHOR

Focusing on art, journaling and poetry, Trevi Bennett has had the opportunity to process and assimilate her work into an observation of the experiment life. After studying in Europe, she graduated with a Bachelor of Fine Arts from the University of Colorado, Boulder, and has shown her water-based oil paintings in California and Colorado. She can be found creating, listening to music, playing, writing, skiing and hiking.

Trevi Bennett's first publication Roses was released in January of 2012, available through Amazon, Kindle and CreateSpace eStore https://www.createspace.com/3746816

www.ingramcontent.com/pod-product-compliance
Lightning Source LLC
Chambersburg PA
CBHW060647030426
42337CB00018B/3497